Kooky Cookery

Written, compiled and field-tested by Bryan Ballinger

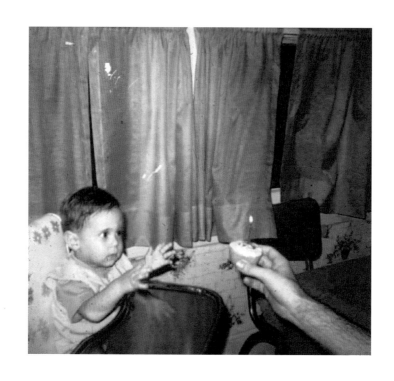

www.kookycookery.com

bryan@kookycookery.com

ISBN-13:
978-1463650896

ISBN-10:
1463650892

This book is dedicated to Susan Goodman and Ben Exworthy.

Special thanks to Jen and Merrill.

TABLE OF CONTENTS

TABLE OF CONTENTS

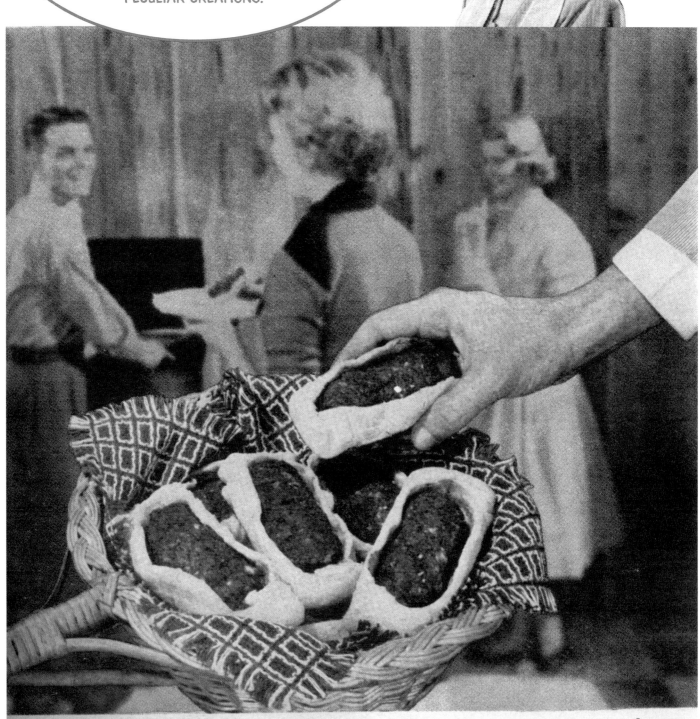

A guest won't say no when hot, crunchy Hamburger Boats are passed again

6

Many of these culinary gems were first published in recipe booklets from the 1930s, 40s, and 50s by corporations trying to invent new ways for housewives to use their products (and, of course, buy more of their products.) Hence, with the enthusiastic lobbying of Jell-O, Royal, and Knox, gelatin became the Swiss army knife of food preparation, used to suspend virtually any combination of ingredients. Food product companies weren't the only ones creating these recipes. Even electric companies got into the act. For example, *Meals Go Modern Electrically* was put out by the National Kitchen Modernizing Bureau, which was sponsored by the Edison Electric Institute and the National Electrical Manufacturers Association. Crazy, complicated entrees were the perfect way to get folks to indulge in the benefits of a new electric oven.

"Before-dinner freedom means a lot to me—so of course I'm enthusiastic about my electric range. Whole meals cook to perfection in the oven while I'm resting or gadding about."

A lot of the recipes also came from food-stretching pamphlets. While many of these recipes did result in dishes rubbery enough to stretch across the table, "food-stretching" refers to making the contents of your pantry last longer. An example would be using oatmeal in meatloaf to help make the recipe feed more people. This was particularly important in times of war, which was when many of these booklets were produced. Stretching often involved meats, using those leftover parts that were—and still are—very hard to incorporate into an edible dish.

THE AMERICAN WOMAN'S 3-way
Meat Stretcher
COOK BOOK

ONE OF THE BIGGEST PUBLISHERS OF THESE STRETCHING RECIPE COLLECTIONS WAS THE CULINARY ARTS INSTITUTE. THEIR RECIPE BOOKLETS WERE SOLD AS PART OF A 24-VOLUME ENCYCLOPEDIA EXTRAVAGANZA OF COOKERY. MANY SUCH BOOKLETS SALUTED HOMEMAKERS NOT ONLY FOR SAVING MONEY, BUT ALSO FOR CONTRIBUTING TO THE WAR EFFORT BY CREATIVELY NOURISHING THEIR FAMILIES.

Published for

One of America's foremost organizations devoted to the science of Better Cookery

WIN WITH FOOD

Food management, one of wartime's most important jobs, rests squarely on the shoulders of the American homemaker. Food will win the war and make the peace *only* if it is administered wisely by the meal planners of the nation, so that supplies will be adequate to meet the ever-increasing demands.

Knowing about food is more essential today than ever before in history. In times like these it is not enough to have a few pet recipes. You have to broaden your food knowledge and honestly look beyond personal tastes and life-time habits, in order to be able to view the food picture as a whole.

You should resolve to get out of that old food rut so that you are ready to meet big shifts in shortages and supplies. You should try to conserve in every way possible. Above all you must choose foods that will provide maximum nourishment, and learn how to prepare them correctly, so as to avoid loss of nutrients through improper cooking. In these ways you will help to assure for your family the energy and good health needed to handle added tasks and stepped-up activities. Here is your chance, too—as a homemaker—to contribute directly to winning the war.

These Cook Books have been prepared to help you not only through present days of readjustment but in happier times to follow—when the lessons in nutrition, thrift and adaptability now being learned will make better food managers of us all.

In the 1940s, many American women entered the workforce to replace the men going off to war. Later, these women needed to be transitioned back into the home to make room for the returning soldiers. What better way to facilitate this exodus than with recipe booklets that glamorized the homemaker-whether by glorifying thrift to help families through shortages, or by preparing meals that thrilled a husband.

It is one thing to use recipes to encourage the use of products and to help women feel better about staying at home. But coming up with such odd food combinations is quite another. Enter the corporate test kitchen and the domestic scientist.

The General Electric Kitchen Institute

Many different kinds of companies had corporate test kitchens-from companies selling rice or bananas to companies making mixers, canning jars, and refrigerators.

A Corner of Frigidaire's Experimental Kitchen

Home Economics Building, Syracuse University

Recipes

DEVELOPED AND TESTED EXCLUSIVELY FOR YOUR HAMILTON BEACH MIXER

The Quik-Mix recipes in these pages were especially developed and tested for use with the Hamilton Beach Food Mixer in the College of Home Economics, Syracuse University, under the direction of Edith H. Nason, Professor of Foods. They have been accepted and are being used in teaching by a large number of home economists. All other recipes in this book were also especially tested at Syracuse University for use with the Hamilton Beach Food Mixer.

Heading up efforts in the corporate kitchen were the domestic scientists. And at the home economic colleges it was usually an esteemed professor of foods.

Domestic science experts pass the recipe for *5-minute Chocolate Frosting* on to their classes with especial pride. Remembering how much trouble beginners *usually* have with frosting, teacher and pupils welcome this fool-proof new way!

They combined culinary creativity with the mandate to develop new ways to use products. Their results speak for themselves. To explain the mysterious nature of these recipes, it helps to look a little closer at what they have in common. There are two main characteristics they all seem to share.

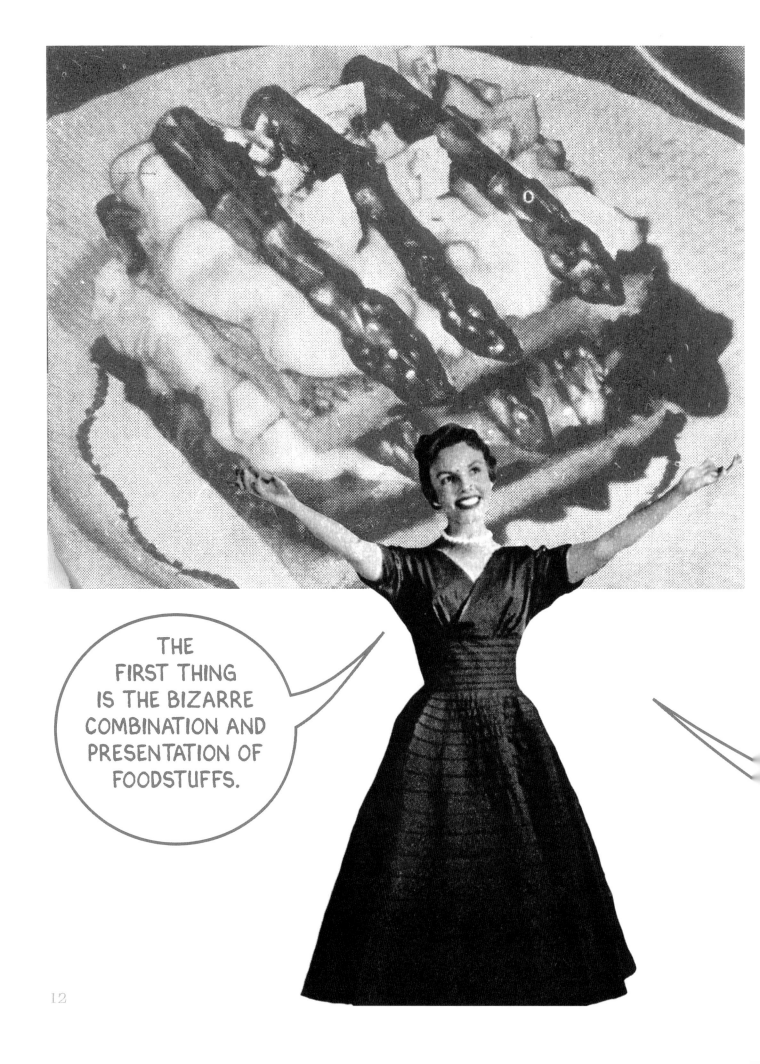

*The French casserole adds
to the beauty of serving*

THE
SECOND THING IS TRULY
UNAPPETIZING PHOTOGRAPHY.

KINGAN'S
RELIABLE

Breakfast Dishes men like..

MANY women are learning—and their number increases daily —that breakfast is important. Men know that the right start must be made to have the right sort of day, and women are realizing that, to discover what their husbands really want for breakfast, and to give it to them, is the beginning of wifely wisdom.

Men like something substantial for breakfast — even more emphatically, it seems, than on every other occasion— and there is nothing more substantial than meat. To vary the egg, toast and coffee menu with delicious ham, bacon or sausage, puts breakfast on the map, and gives a man the reassuring feeling that he is "going places"—and going with proper and satisfying attention to his inner man. We offer you several suggestions for breakfast dishes which men like, and which we hope you will promptly appropriate and make your own, for we are sure you will like them too.

BREAKFAST AND LUNCH ARE TWO OF THE MOST IMPORTANT MEALS OF THE DAY. THESE RECIPES WERE DESIGNED TO GET YOUR MORNING OR AFTERNOON OFF TO A DIGESTIBLE IF NOT DELICIOUS START.

Cheese-Burger Pancakes

⅔ cup ground beef
1 cup evaporated milk
½ cup water
1 egg
2 tablespoons melted
shortening

1 cup sifted all-purpose
flour
2 tablespoons cornmeal
2 teaspoons baking
powder
Zippy Cheese Sauce

Soak meat in evaporated milk 5 to 10 minutes, breaking apart with fork. Beat in water, egg, and shortening. Sift together the dry ingredients; blend in meat mixture. Spoon onto lightly greased griddle and spread into 4-inch rounds. Brown on both sides. Top with Zippy Cheese Sauce. Makes twelve 4-inch pancakes.

Zippy Cheese Sauce: Use 1 roll (6 oz.) garlic- or bacon-flavored process cheese. Combine with 1 can cream of mushroom soup and stir over low heat until cheese melts.

IT'S NOT JUST A PANCAKE; IT'S A MEAL.

New with SPAM! New with Bisquick! "SPAM CAKES"!

SPAM BAKES RIGHT IN THE MIDDLE. This is fun! Both in the making and the eating. The folks'll love these tender golden Bisquick pancakes . . . each one centered with a sizzling slice of SPAM. Here's how you do it:

MAKE BISQUICK PANCAKE BATTER (directions on the box).

BROWN SPAM SLICES ON GRIDDLE . . . 2 to 3 inches apart.

TURN SPAM SLICES . . . pour batter over each slice. Turn again.

. . . And there you are, with big hungry-size pancakes . . . a savory SPAM slice baked right in the middle!

Just be sure it's SPAM you get . . . the famous Hormel blend of sweet juicy pork shoulder and mild tender ham.

And be sure there's plenty of Bisquick, because this is just a sample of all you can do with it.

INSTANT MEAT + INSTANT PANCAKES = A MATCH MADE IN CONVENIENCE.

Broiled Bologna slices will curl into cups; fill with peas and alternate with tomato wedges around rice

BOLOGNA CUPS WITH PEAS

6 slices Bologna, cut ⅛ inch thick
2 tablespoons fat
2 cups cooked peas
1 tomato, cut into wedges
2 cups hot cooked rice

Spread Bologna with fat and broil. As slices heat they will curl into cups. Fill with hot peas, and arrange cups alternately with tomato wedges around rice heaped in center. Garnish, if desired, with sliced hard-cooked egg and green pepper rings. Serves 6.

YOU CALL THAT A CUP? WHAT A BUNCH OF BOLOGNA.

19

2 cups water
½ teaspoon salt
Pepper
½ tablespoon vinegar
1 egg
Hot buttered toast

Heat water to simmering in a shallow pan; add salt, pepper and vinegar. Break egg into a cup and slip it carefully into water. Make a whirlpool with spoon or fork. Let egg cook below boiling point for about 5 minutes or until white is firm and a film has formed over yolk. Remove egg with skimmer, drain and serve on toast or rusk.

TO SERVE POACHED EGGS—
CORNED BEEF HASH— Place eggs on top corned beef hash patties.

Back up the luncheon egg by poaching in meat nests like browned corned beef hash

IS THERE A WORSE WORD COMBINATION THAN "MEAT" AND "NESTS?"

Stuffed Luncheon Loaf

meat jacket

A slick trick, this loaf with its luncheon meat jacket around macaroni-and-cheese filling! It's a make-ahead to bake later.

1 package (7 oz.) elbow macaroni
1 can (12 oz.) ham-pork luncheon
  meat
1 cup diced process cheddar cheese
1 cup soft bread crumbs
2 tablespoons diced pimiento
1 tablespoon onion juice
½ teaspoon salt
¼ teaspoon pepper
1 can cream of chicken soup,
  undiluted
¼ cup coarsely broken cashew nuts

Cook macaroni according to package directions. Drain thoroughly. Cut luncheon meat into 10 thin slices. Trim slices to fit 3-inch depth of loaf pan. Line greased 9- by 5- by 3-inch baking pan with meat slices —4 slices on bottom, 2 on each side, and 1 slice on each end. Dice trimmings and add to macaroni. Combine macaroni with remaining ingredients. Spoon into meat-lined pan. Refrigerate, if desired. Bake in moderate oven (350°) for 30 minutes. Remove from oven and let stand for 5 minutes. Unmold carefully on warmed platter.

21

A striking way to serve a new, colorful and delicious array of sandwich fillings! Just be sure you spread the bread and make the fillings with creamy-smooth Real Mayonnaise, Hellmann's, of course! Extra delicate and light, Hellmann's highlights the natural flavors of other foods, never hides them.

TO ASSEMBLE FLOWER POT:

Cut two 3-1/2", one 3" and two 2-1/2" rounds from 5 bread slices. Spread with Real Mayonnaise, then with filling (about 1/2 cup per sandwich). Stack, use smallest rounds on bottom.

For flowers, insert food picks or skewers into radishes, cherry tomatoes, olives, cucumber or carrot slices. For leaves, use celery, parsley or green pepper.

CHEESE SALAD FILLING:
1/2 pound Swiss cheese, finely shredded (about 2 cups)
1/2 cup chopped tomato
3 tablespoons chopped pimiento stuffed green olives
2 tablespoons chopped green pepper
1/2 cup HELLMANN'S Real Mayonnaise
Salt

Combine ingredients. Makes 2 cups of filling.

I'LL HAVE A SIDE OF MIRACLE-GRO WITH THAT, PLEASE.

FLOWER
POT
SANDWICHES

23

BENEDICTISH FRANKWICHES

SHOWER CAPS FOR YOUR EXPOSED BRAIN? NOPE, IT'S BENEDICTISH FRANKWICHES!

Tomato Buns: Split English muffins; toast in broiler. Spread with butter or margarine. Top each half with 2 tomato slices; 1 split frank, halved; and 1 packaged-cheese slice. Broil.

Combo: Split frank (hot or cold); place between 2 slices buttered white or rye bread or toast. Top with one of these combinations:

Crushed pineapple, apple butter, or applesauce

Sliced, hard-cooked eggs and mayonnaise

Cream cheese and chopped ripe olives

Prepared mustard and orange marmalade

Chili sauce and lettuce or pickle relish

Egg-salad mixture and water cress

Slices cheese, tomato, and onion

Benedictish: Top toasted, split English muffins with frank slices. Then top with poached eggs and hollandaise sauce. Or top with cheese slice; sprinkle with monosodium glutamate. Broil until cheese melts.

Yankee Doodle Pizza Pie

pizza sauce

Blend together 1 (8 oz.) can ANN PAGE Spaghetti Sauce, 1 (7 oz.) can tomato paste, and ¼ teaspoon oregano.

quick crust

Take one package refrigerator biscuits, separate them and press, pat and flatten to line one 12 inch pizza pan (round or square shallow baking pan may be used). Scallop the edge or make a rim.

to put together

Spread about 1½ cups sauce over crust, sprinkle on ½ cup grated Parmesan cheese. Add remaining sauce to 1 can (21 to 23 ozs.) of ANN PAGE BEANS (any style) pour over cheese layer. Decorate center with ¼ pound grated Mozarrella cheese and green pepper rings. Bake in hot oven (425° F.) 10 minutes; then at 325 degrees for 20-25 minutes more. Serve with Italian sausage, pimento, or anchovy.

Backwoods Sandwich Loaf

1 loaf unsliced bread
Mayonnaise or salad dressing
1 6-oz. pkg. soft pimento cheese
1 can chunk-style tuna (1 cup)
1 large tomato, sliced
3 finely chopped, hard-cooked
   eggs
2 3-oz. cans deviled ham
Chunk-style peanut butter

Cut loaf lengthwise, crust and all, into 7 layers. Spread each with mayonnaise. Working from the bottom up, fill each layer with the following: Cheese spread; tuna, mixed with mayonnaise; tomato slices, sprinkled with salt and pepper; egg, mixed with mayonnaise; deviled ham; peanut butter. Top with crust, pressing down firmly. Refrigerate if desired. Slice into ¾"-thick slices.

Makes 10 servings

TOO BAD THEY LEFT OUT THE PHOTO WITH THIS RECIPE. MAYBE THEY SHOULD HAVE LEFT OUT THE INGREDIENTS.

Crispy, browned cheese ball appetizers are a happy surprise to almost everyone

2 egg whites
1 cup grated American cheese
Dash of cayenne
¼ cup grated dry bread crumbs

Beat egg whites stiff, add cheese, cayenne and bread crumbs. Pat into small balls and fry in hot deep fat (375° F.) until light brown. Makes about 16 balls.

TO EAT OR TO LANCE, THAT IS THE QUESTION.

29

CRISP ROLL CUPS

4 long crisp rolls
1 cup minced cooked chicken
6 tablespoons India relish
4 drops Worcestershire sauce
2 tablespoons salad dressing
½ teaspoon grated onion
¼ teaspoon salt
8 stuffed olives, sliced

Cut off ends 2 inches long from rolls. Remove soft center from ends and fill hollow with mixture of remaining ingredients. Slice a stuffed olive and place in overlapping slices on each cup or garnish with sieved egg yolks. Serve on hors d'oeuvres picks. Makes 8 cups.

Fill roll cups with any of fillings for Stuffed Eggs (page 16) instead of chicken filling.

COLD SHRIMP HORS D'OEUVRES

8 canned or fresh cleaned shrimp
8 rounds bread
¼ cup mayonnaise
8 drops Worcestershire sauce
Curry powder, Parsley

Place shrimp on round of bread cut the same size. Top each shrimp with mayonnaise, season with Worcestershire sauce and a dash of curry powder. Garnish with sprig of parsley. Makes 8 hors d'oeuvres.

STUFFED CABBAGE HEAD

1 head cabbage
Sour cream dressing
16 gherkins
16 cocktail frankfurters

Wash cabbage and remove outside leaves. Cut a slice from top and remove center leaving a shell. Shred cabbage from center, mix thoroughly with cream dressing, and chill. When ready to serve fill center with shredded cabbage. Spear gherkins and sausages on hors d'oeuvres picks and stick picks on outside of cabbage head, alternating gherkins and frankfurters. Serve with butter crackers or salted wafers.

Use cooked shrimp marinated in French dressing instead of frankfurters.

Fill center with chicken, shrimp or crab-meat salad, saving center cabbage to be served creamed or fried. Garnish with stuffed or ripe olives on picks.

SHRIMP À LA SANTA

3 cups finely chopped, cooked shrimp
1¼ cups Triscuit Wafers crumbs, finely rolled
2 eggs, beaten
1 clove garlic, chopped
¼ cup melted butter or margarine

Mix shrimp, Triscuit Wafers crumbs and eggs. Shape into small balls. Sauté garlic and shrimp balls in butter until brown. Discard garlic. Serve shrimp balls immediately with new, new, subtly onion-tasting French Onion Thins and crunchy-crisp, delicious Triscuit Wafers.

SANTA NEEDS SOME WART REMOVER.

Sparkling and refreshing Tomato Aspic adds a bright touch to any meal with its shimmering goodness.

INGREDIENTS

- 1 envelope Knox Unflavored Gelatine
- 1 ¾ cups tomato juice, divided
- ¼ teaspoon salt
- ½ teaspoon sugar
- ½ teaspoon Worcestershire sauce
- ⅛ teaspoon Tabasco
- 2 tablespoons lemon juice

ENOUGH WITH THE SHIMMERING GOODNESS. BRING ON THE QUIVERING RESILIENCY.

2 packages (3 oz. each) or
   1 package (6 oz.) Jell-O
   Lemon Gelatin
1 tablespoon salt
2 cups boiling water
2 cups cold water
2 tablespoons vinegar
1½ cups finely shredded carrots
1¾ cups finely shredded cabbage
1 teaspoon minced chives
1½ cups finely chopped spinach

Dissolve Jell-O Gelatin and salt in boiling water. Add cold water and vinegar. Chill until slightly thickened. Divide into three portions. Fold carrots into one portion; pour into a 9x5x3-inch loaf pan. Chill until set, but not firm. Fold cabbage into second portion. Pour into pan; chill until set, but not firm. Fold chives and spinach into remaining gelatin. Pour into pan. Chill until firm. Unmold. Slice and garnish with crisp greens. Makes about 6 cups, or 12 side salads.

VEGETABLE TRIO

A dazzling, delicious rainbow of fresh vegetables for your dinner table.

DARLING,
COULD YOU CARVE THE SALAD,
PLEASE?

35

Hot bacon dressing the way grandfather liked it

BACON DRESSING

3 slices bacon, diced
¼ cup vinegar
2 tablespoons water
1 tablespoon sugar
½ teaspoon salt
Dash pepper
1 hard-cooked egg, chopped

Fry bacon until crisp. Add remaining ingredients. Pour immediately over salad greens. Makes about ⅔ cup.

WHAT DO YOU DO WITH THAT LEFTOVER BACON GREASE? MIX IT TOGETHER WITH VINEGAR AND SERVE IT TO GRANDPA!

JELLIED LAWN CLUMP

A new and deliciously different twist for a popular stand-by — green salad is molded for added pleasure.

INGREDIENTS

1 envelope Knox Unflavored Gelatine	1 tablespoon lemon juice
1 tablespoon sugar	¼ cup chopped scallions
1 teaspoon salt	1 cup shredded raw spinach
⅛ teaspoon pepper	1 cup chopped celery
1¾ cups water, divided	¼ cup shredded raw carrots
¼ cup vinegar	

FOLLOW THE RECIPE, OR JUST KICK ONE OUT OF YOUR MOWER.

Are you a corned beef and cabbage fan? You'll like this appetizing layered salad, a new way to serve the combination.

INGREDIENTS

Cabbage Layer

- 1 envelope Knox Unflavored Gelatine
- 2 tablespoons sugar
- ½ teaspoon salt
- 1¼ cups water, divided
- 2 tablespoons lemon juice
- ¼ cup vinegar
- 2 tablespoons chopped green pepper
- 2 cups finely shredded cabbage

Corned Beef Layer

- 1 envelope Knox Unflavored Gelatine
- ½ cup water
- 2 tablespoons lemon juice
- ¼ teaspoon salt
- ¾ cup mayonnaise
- ¼ cup minced onion
- ½ cup chopped sweet pickle
- ½ cup diced celery
- 1 can (12 oz.) corned beef, finely cut

1 TO PREPARE CABBAGE LAYER Mix gelatine, sugar and salt thoroughly in a small saucepan.

2 Add ½ cup of the water. Place over low heat, stirring constantly until gelatine is dissolved.

3 Remove from heat and stir in remaining ¾ cup water, lemon juice and vinegar. Chill mixture to unbeaten egg white consistency.

4 Fold in green pepper and cabbage. Turn into an 8-inch square pan and chill until almost firm.

5 TO PREPARE CORNED BEEF LAYER Sprinkle gelatine on cold water to soften.

6 Place over low heat and stir until gelatine is dissolved.

7 Remove from heat and stir in lemon juice and salt; cool. Gradually add mayonnaise.

8 Mix in remaining ingredients. Turn on top of almost firm first layer and chill until firm.

9 Unmold on board; cut into squares and place on serving platter. Serve with mayonnaise.

39

250 WAYS TO PREPARE *Meat*

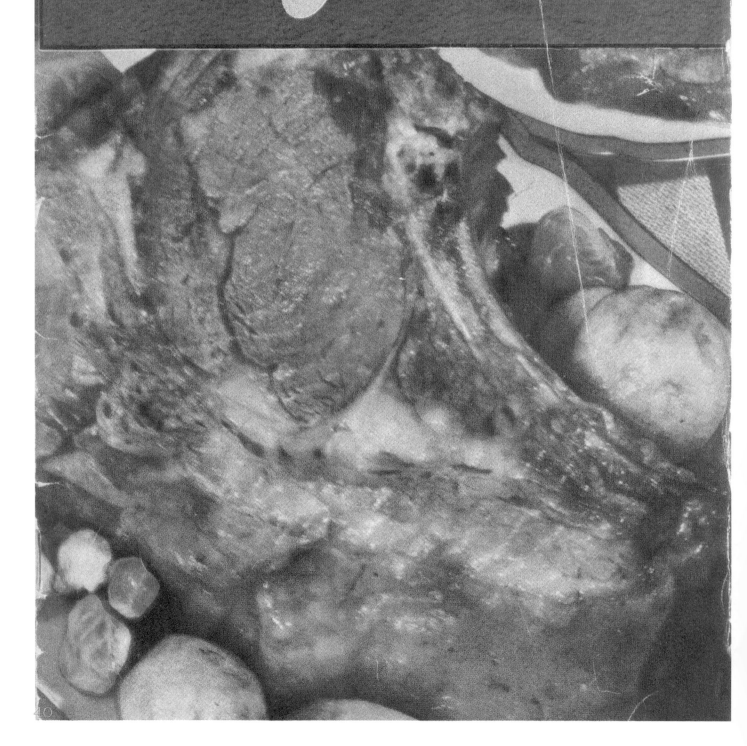

KINGAN'S
RELIABLE

Meat : Nature's most healthful food

Man's appetite for meat is instinctive and universal; meat decidedly is not a food for which a taste has to be "cultivated." It is a natural taste. Moreover, above all other foods, it is unquestionably the most sustaining. But many people do not realize that meat is also nature's most *healthful* food.

From the standpoint of health, there has been more or less vague prejudice against meat in favor of a purely vegetarian diet. But the cult of vegetarianism is fading into the obscure region of exploded theories, retreating, like so many theories, before the facts of sounder scientific knowledge.

Many medical authorities now state that in order to properly balance a diet, meat must be included, and they tell us that meat contains vital nutritive elements, which are more easily assimilated, than any other food. We offer in this booklet delicious recipes for the serving of Kingan's Meats, with the hope that it will prove a welcome aid to the homemaker in the art of menu planning. Meat is the *piece de resistance* of every meal—and for almost a century Kingan's Meats have been synonymous with quality, and the highest standards in preparation and packaging. When you buy Kingan's Reliable Meats, you can rest assured that you have secured the best.

Ann King
HOME ECONOMICS DIRECTOR
KINGAN & COMPANY

n U. S. A

> WITH THE BLIGHT THAT WAS THE "CULT OF VEGETARIANISM" FINALLY GONE, WE NOW PRESENT A GALLERY OF "HEALTHFUL" RECIPES THAT PACK A DELIGHTFULLY MEATY PUNCH.

41

Fricadellons utilize those oddments of cooked meat in such a way the family will wish there were more

FRICADELLONS

1 large onion, chopped
2 tablespoons fat
1 cup dry bread softened in water
2 cups cooked ground meat
1 egg
2 tablespoons chopped parsley
1/8 teaspoon allspice
1/4 teaspoon salt
Dash pepper

Brown onion lightly in 1 tablespoon fat in skillet. Press water from bread; add onion, meat, egg and seasonings. Mix well. Shape into flat cakes and sauté until crisp in remaining fat. Serves 4. If desired arrange cooked noodles in a ring, fill center with cooked vegetables and border with the fricadellons.

Combine all ingredients, add 2 additional eggs and pack into a greased ring mold. Bake at 325°F. 1 hour or until firm.

WE'LL JUST TELL THE KIDS IT'S "HAMBURGER."

Pan-fry breaded brains to a delicate golden brown and garnish with sliced tomatoes

WHEN IT COMES TO BRAINS, BREADED IS ALWAYS BETTER THAN BATTERED.

BREADED BRAINS

1½ pounds brains, precooked
1 egg, beaten
2 tablespoons cold water
1 teaspoon salt
⅛ teaspoon pepper
Bread crumbs or cracker meal
2 tablespoons fat

Roll brains in egg which has been mixed with cold water. Dip in seasoned crumbs and brown in hot fat in skillet. Serves 6.

43

Egg and olive slices, glimmering under aspic, dress up the veal from yesterday's roast

QUITE DELICIOUS. JUST DON'T LET IT NEAR YOUR FACE.

JELLIED VEAL LOAF

1 (10½-ounce) can condensed
    chicken soup
3 cups ground cooked veal
2 teaspoons unflavored gelatin
2 tablespoons water
¾ teaspoon salt
⅛ teaspoon pepper
1 hard-cooked egg, sliced
5 stuffed olives, sliced

Strain chicken soup and heat broth. Mix rice, chicken and celery from soup with veal and grind. Soften gelatin in cold water 5 minutes; dissolve in hot broth; mix with ground meat mixture, salt and pepper. Cool until beginning to thicken. Arrange egg and olive slices in bottom of loaf pan. Pour meat mixture on garnish; chill until firm. Unmold on lettuce or greens. Serves 6.

To have pattern show, pour a thin layer of clear gelatin on bottom of pan. When firm arrange egg and olives on it and cover with ¼-inch layer of clear gelatin. Combine remaining gelatin as above.

Ham Loaf

3 slices bread (dried or fresh)
¼ cup Daricraft
1½ cups ground ham (fresh or leftover)
1½ cups (1 pound) ground veal
1 chopped onion
1 unbeaten egg
¾ cup water
¾ cup vinegar
1 cup brown sugar
1 tablespoon ground mustard
Dash ground cloves

Crumble bread in mixing bowl, add Daricraft and mix as for dressing. Add to this the ground ham, ground veal and onion and egg and make into loaf and stick top with whole cloves. Mix water, vinegar, sugar and ground mustard together and pour over meat loaf.

Bake at 350° for 45 minutes, basting frequently with sauce.

IT'S ALL A QUESTION OF SCALE.

46

BEEHIVE SALAD

BOIL until tender { 48 nine-inch strips macaroni (*6 ounces*) *in* 8 cups boiling water 2 teaspoons salt

Drain, rinse and dry on towel.

Heat to boiling point { 10½-oz. can condensed tomato soup ¼ cup vinegar ½ teaspoon salt ⅛ teaspoon pepper

Add and stir until dissolved......... { 1 package lemon-flavored gelatin

Chill until mixture begins to thicken.

Rub with vegetable oil an 8-inch mold having sloping sides.

Line mold with strips of unbroken macaroni, using 24 strips.

Chop remaining macaroni:

Add to chopped macaroni......... { ¾ cup Pet Milk 1½ cups boiled or baked ham,* *diced* (¾ *lb.*)

Fold into gelatin mixture. Pour into mold being careful to keep the macaroni against sides of mold. Chill until firm. Unmold and cut into slices. . . . *Serves 8.*

*Tongue or corned beef, either freshly cooked or canned, may be substituted for the boiled or baked ham.

A CUTAWAY VIEW OF SOME ANCIENT POTTERY HOLDING THE ASHEN REMAINS OF A LONG-DEAD KING? NO SILLY, IT'S DINNER!

47

ECONOMICAL RICELAND RICE MEAT LOAF
(Illustrated below)

1 medium-sized onion, chopped
1 cup cooked Riceland Rice
1 pound ground smoked ham
1 pound ground veal
2 beaten eggs
1½ cups milk
1/8 teaspoon pepper

1 teaspoon salt
½ teaspoon garlic salt

TOPPING:
1/3 cup brown sugar
1/4 cup vinegar
1 tablespoon dry mustard

Mix first 4 ingredients for loaf together, beat eggs into milk and add to meat. Add the pepper, salt and garlic salt. This makes a soft mixture. Pour into well greased loaf pan and pat down so top is even. Combine brown sugar, vinegar and mustard. Pour over top of loaf and bake 1½ hours at 250°F. Garnish with cooked onions. Serve with sauce, ketchup or gravy if desired. This recipe makes 6 to 8 servings.

Save Money! Use Riceland Rice as a Meat Extender

By using economical, nourishing Riceland Rice as a meat extender—in meat loaves, hamburgers and stews—you can save a lot of money on your food budget. Riceland Rice carries and extends the luscious meat flavor. Try this economical Riceland Rice Meat Loaf and see!

Budget Tip: To save even more money on your food budget—use more Riceland Rice and less meat in the above recipe.

49

Creamed chicken takes on a new glamour when it appears in a noodle or rice ring

1 tablespoon parsley
2 cups diced cooked chicken
1 cup medium white sauce
1 egg yolk
2 tablespoons milk

Add parsley and chicken to white sauce and heat. Beat egg yolk, adding milk and pour into mixture. Cook for 2 minutes, stirring constantly. Serve in ring or in croustades. Serves 6.

Mushrooms or chopped cooked eggs, chopped pimientos and olives may be added.

IF ONLY
EVERYTHING COULD TAKE ON
SUCH GLAMOUR SO EFFORTLESSLY.

51

MOLDED CHICKEN CRANBERRY LOAF

Part 1

1 (1-pound) can or jar jellied cranberry sauce
½ cup water
1 tablespoon unflavored gelatin
2 tablespoons cold water

Crush cranberry sauce with fork; add water and heat. Soften gelatin in cold water 5 minutes; dissolve in hot cranberry sauce. Pour into loaf pan which has been dipped in cold water. Chill until firm.

Part 2

2 teaspoons unflavored gelatin
½ cup cold water
2 cups diced cooked chicken
½ cup diced celery
¼ cup minced green pepper
½ teaspoon salt

Soften gelatin in cold water 5 minutes; dissolve over boiling water. Add chicken, celery, green pepper and salt. Pour on top of firm cranberry jelly. Chill until firm; unmold. Garnish with olives and lettuce cups filled with mayonnaise. Serves 6.

The ruby sheen of jellied cranberries high-lights this holiday supper loaf of molded chicken in a happy combination of color and flavor

AND A HAPPY COMBINATION OF SHEEN AND MOLDEDNESS, TOO!

Chicken and Vegetables in Aspic

1 package Royal Gelatin Aspic
1 cup boiling water
1 cup cold water
4 slices smoked tongue

4 slices white meat of chicken
1 cup diced carrots, cooked
1 cup lima beans

Dissolve Royal Gelatin Aspic in boiling water; add cold water. Chill until it begins to thicken; pour thin layer in loaf pan; arrange on this overlapping slices of chicken and tongue alternately. Add vegetables to remaining gelatin mixture and pour carefully on top of meat layer. Chill until firm. Unmould and garnish with salad greens. Serves 8.

53

1 package (3 oz.) Jell-O Lemon
   or Orange-Pineapple Gelatir
½ teaspoon salt
1¾ cups boiling chicken broth*
   Dash of cayenne
2 tablespoons vinegar
⅓ cup whipping cream
⅓ cup mayonnaise
1 cup diced cooked chicken*
1 cup finely chopped celery
1 tablespoon chopped pimiento

*Or use 1¾ cups boiling water with 2 chicken bouillon cubes and 1 can (6 oz.) boned chicken, drained and diced.

Dissolve Jell-O Gelatin and salt in boiling broth. Add cayenne and vinegar; chill until very thick. Whip the cream. Fold cream and mayonnaise into gelatin, blending well. Then fold in remaining ingredients. Pour into a 1-quart mold or individual molds. Chill until firm. Unmold. Makes 4 cups, or 4 entree servings.

A hearty flavorful entree for hot summer or busy, meeting-filled days.

NOTHING SAYS A WORKING LUNCH LIKE A RING OF VINEGAR, CHICKEN, AND LEMON JELLO.

HOTDOGS AND SAUSAGES AREN'T MEANT TO STAND ON THEIR OWN. THEY NEED TO BE GUSSIED UP TO MEET A GUEST'S EXPECTATIONS OF A MAIN COURSE. THESE RECIPES ARE HERE TO HELP.

Frank 'n' Bean Bake

(Pictured on page 45)

3 No. 3 cans baked beans with pork
¾ cup catchup
¾ cup minced onion
4½ teasp. prepared mustard
¾ teasp. Worcestershire
2½ lbs. franks

Start heating oven to 350°F. Combine beans with catchup, onion, mustard, and Worcestershire. Add franks, then turn into electric roaster or roasting pan and bake 25 to 30 min.

To serve: Arrange Frank 'n' Bean Bake on buffet table with a green salad, rolls, and a variety of relishes.

Makes 10 to 12 servings

WHICH IS MORE AWKWARD—PUTTING THEM IN, OR TAKING THEM OUT?

BACON-BOUND WEINER WREATH

A crown roast of wieners is an ideal solution for guest problems when the budget is low

...BUT
THE DIRECTIONS ARE
WORSE.

STUFFED CROWN ROAST OF FRANKFURTERS

20 frankfurters
2 cups cooked sauerkraut

Arrange frankfurters side by side, with curved side up. Using large needle and string, sew through all the frankfurters ½ inch from the bottom and ½ inch from the top. Tie ends of top string together, bringing first and last frankfurter of the row together. Repeat with bottom string. Stand frankfurters on end to form a crown. (Concave side should be out.) Fill center of crown with sauerkraut. Bake filled crown in moderate oven (375°F.) about 20 minutes. Serves 10.

Fill crown with stuffing, creamed cabbage, creamed cauliflower or potato balls instead of sauerkraut.

Spaghetti ... WITH SAUSAGE-STUFFED APPLES

½ lb. cooked American Beauty
    Spaghetti
6 apples, medium size

6 link sausage
2 tablespoons butter
Salt and pepper

Wash and core apples, filling cavity with sausage link. Set in pan, cover bottom with water and bake until apples are tender; drain. Heat butter in skillet; brown spaghetti lightly. Season to taste. Serves four to six persons.

THEY WON'T STOP LOOKING AT ME.

Stuffed Frankfurters

(pictured at right)

2 cups mashed potato — make with:
- 1½ cups water
- ½ teaspoon salt
- ½ cup milk
- ½ cup French's Instant Potato powder
- ¼ cup chopped parsley

- ¼ cup minced onion
- 1 tablespoon chopped pimiento
- ⅛ teaspoon French's Black Pepper
- 1 tablespoon melted butter or margarine
- French's Cream Salad Mustard
- 8 Frankfurters

Prepare mashed potato (approximately 2 cups) using first four ingredients listed in this recipe. Mix as outlined on the French's Instant Potato package. Add parsley, onion, pimiento and pepper. Cover frankfurters with boiling water and allow to stand 8 minutes. Split frankfurters lengthwise, spread with mustard. Stuff frankfurters with first mixture. Brush with melted butter. Place on broiler rack. Broil 10 minutes or until delicately browned.

ARE TURKEY HOTDOGS EASIER TO STUFF?

Fish, when properly prepared, offers nourishment, satisfaction and menu variety. Food from water is still a good buy, despite higher price tickets, because in times of shortages it is more than ever important to choose foods that provide the maximum of nourishment. And now that fish is unrationed it is unquestionably in the swim and every homemaker will want to know how to buy and prepare it. Luckily there are plenty of fish in the sea and here are plenty of ways to cook them!

FISH COME IN SO MANY DIFFERENT SHAPES AND SIZES. AND THAT'S BEFORE THEY'RE PUT INTO THE HANDS OF A DOMESTIC SCIENTIST. IT'S NO WONDER THAT THE SEAFOOD RECIPES PRESENTED HERE ARE SOME OF THE MOST VISUALLY BIZARRE. TAKE A DEEP BREATH, OR JUST HOLD YOUR NOSE, AND DIVE RIGHT IN.

First step in preparation of a molded salad is to have all ingredients ready

When gelatine mixture is partially thickened it goes into an attractive fish mold

Garnish the unmolded salad colorfully, and serve with plenty of real mayonnaise

GLACE FISH MOLD
(Pictured here)

½ cup cold water
1 envelope plain gelatine
1 cup boiling water
2 tablespoons sugar
½ teaspoon salt
3 tablespoons lemon juice

1 cup flaked fish*
¼ cup diced green pepper
½ unpeeled cucumber, cut
1 small onion, sliced
½ cup chopped pimiento

¼ cup diced celery

Soften gelatine in cold water, dissolve in boiling water. Add sugar, salt, lemon juice. Cool. When mixture begins to thicken, fold in fish, green pepper, cucumber wedges, onion rings, pimiento and celery. Pour into 1-quart mold, rinsed in cold water. When firm, unmold, garnish as desired, and serve with bowl of real mayonnaise.

*Use any flaked cooked fish or shellfish.

FAUX
INTERNAL ORGANS
AND WALLEYES. WHO KNEW THE
COMMON HOUSEHOLD OLIVE WAS SO
VERSATILE?

TUNA PLANKED STEAK

½ cup chopped celery
½ cup minced onion
1½ teasp. salt   ¼ teasp. pepper
1 cup milk   3 cups bread crumbs
2 7-oz. tins Breast-O'-Chicken fancy tuna
   (or Breast-O'-Chicken Chunk Pack)
3 tablesp. fat
1 12-oz. pkg. fresh frozen peas
6 whole spiced peaches
6 slices tomatoes

Cook celery until tender; add minced onion, salt and pepper. Add milk to bread crumbs. Combine two mixtures and add Breast-O'-Chicken tuna. Pour into hot fat in skillet; cook 15 min. Turn onto steak plank. Use pastry bag to spread mashed potatoes around steak and make nests for peas. Place in oven at 400°F. until potatoes brown. Place peaches and tomatoes around steak. Serves 6.

MANY very unusual recipes for delicious meals can be made using Breast-O'-Chicken Brand tuna. They are not nearly as difficult as they look in an illustration. It's nice to serve something different occasionally. Try this tuna planked steak recipe.

IT MIGHT BE EASIER TO MAKE THAN IT LOOKS, BUT IS IT EASIER TO EAT THAN IT LOOKS?

Whole hard-cooked eggs in this jellied tuna loaf add a gay and decorative note

1 tablespoon unflavored gelatin
¼ cup cold water
1½ cups hot seasoned stock

Soften gelatin in cold water. Dissolve in hot stock. Add any of following mixtures when gelatin begins to thicken. Pour into desired mold and chill until firm. Unmold and garnish with **vegetable** curls or cups, radish **roses**, endive or parsley.

JELLIED TUNA—Omit stock. Use ½ cup water. Combine with 2 cups flaked tuna, 1 cup mayonnaise and ¼ cup minced sweet pickles.

MAKE SURE YOUR PRESENTATION SHOWS OFF THE MYSTERIOUS AND DECORATIVE INNER CORE.

...THE MOST BEAUTIFUL CAKE I EVER BAKED... FROM MY OWN RECIPE, TOO!

Smart girl, Sally. She knows men's weakness for chocolate cake. And when he says, "Say, some cook, you are! Why, not even my mother can make frosting like this!", Sally blushes modestly and holds her tongue. Why should she tell him that with her magic recipe, 'most any little dumb Dora can now make grand frosting! A girl has to keep some things to herself!

IT'S ALWAYS BEST TO TAKE A MILITARY APPROACH TO CULINARY STRATEGY. PLAN YOUR MEALS LIKE A BATTLE. WHEN YOU GET TO THE END, IF THINGS HAVEN'T GONE WELL, HIT THEM WITH THE GUT BOMB.

Yum! youngsters just love 'em
airplane bananas with fudge sauce

No cooking for this dessert—treat that really thrills (and fills). All you need is a banana per person, some fudge sauce and a few sugar wafers (photo shows Nabisco). The cream clouds are optional.

IF YOUR GUESTS BALK, YOU CAN ALWAYS BLAME THE DOG.

STEAMED PRUNE PUDDING

1½ cups cooked SUNSWEET Prunes
⅓ cup shortening
1 cup brown sugar (packed)
1 egg
2 cups sifted all-purpose flour
3 teaspoons baking powder
1 teaspoon salt
1 teaspoon cinnamon
½ teaspoon allspice
¼ teaspoon nutmeg
¾ cup cooking liquid from prunes
½ cup mixed candied fruits
½ cup chopped walnuts

Pit prunes and chop. Cream shortening and sugar together thoroughly. Blend in lightly beaten egg. Sift together flour, baking powder, salt and spice. Add to creamed mixture alternately with prune liquid. Stir in prunes, candied fruits and nuts. Turn into well-greased 1½-quart mold. Cover tightly and place in kettle containing enough hot water to cover ⅔ of mold. Steam 2½ hours. Let stand 5 minutes, then turn out of mold. Serve hot with hard sauce. Serves 10 to 12.

Hard Sauce: Cream ¼ cup butter and 1 cup sifted confectioners' sugar together thoroughly. Add 1 or 2 tablespoons brandy, or ½ teaspoon vanilla and 2 teaspoons hot water. Stir until smooth and fluffy. Makes about 1 cup.
Illustrated on page 34.

GO AHEAD, CHOW DOWN HARD. IT'LL ALWAYS LAND SOFT..

MAGIC!

You make this pudding without opening the can!

MAGIC CARAMEL PUDDING

(Caramelized Eagle Brand)

Place one or more unopened cans of Eagle Brand Sweetened Condensed Milk in a kettle of boiling water and keep at boiling point for 3 hours. CAUTION — Be sure to keep can well covered with water.

Oh, Yes, They'll Just "Pop In" for a Pot-Luck Dinner, but those too-casual in-laws of yours will expect something good. And you can be ready. Just boil several cans of Eagle Brand (unopened, mind you! See page 10) and open them up as needed. You'll find a beautiful shining mold of Caramel Pudding inside. Actually! Slice it, garnish it, and serve it with nonchalance. It's gur-rand! And—*P.S.*—there's nothing but Eagle Brand in it, so it costs next to nothing.

A HUSH FELL OVER THE GATHERED GUESTS AS DESSERT SLOWLY SLID OUT OF THE CAN.

Drain well. . . . . { 1½ cups sliced peaches,* canned or fresh

Save juice to use in beverages or sauces.

Reserve ½ cup peaches to garnish mold.

Push remaining peaches through a sieve. There should be ¾ cup.

Fold into peach pulp. . . . . { 14 marshmallows, *cut in small pieces* 1 teaspoon grated lemon rind ¼ teaspoon salt

Chill.

Dissolve. . . . . { 1 package lemon-flavored gelatin *in* 1 cup boiling water

Cool thoroughly, then stir in { ¾ cup Pet Milk

Chill until mixture begins to thicken.

Rub with vegetable oil a loaf pan or mold holding about 4 cups.

Cut into ½ inch strips. . . . . . { 2 marshmallows

Garnish bottom of oiled pan with marshmallow strips and reserved peach slices.

Whip chilled gelatin mixture with rotary egg beater until fluffy. Fold in peach and marshmallow mixture. Put into prepared pan. Chill until firm. Unmold and serve at once. . . . *Serves 8.*

Only by using cream could the rich flavor and grand texture of this dessert be duplicated. But cream costs much more than Irradiated Pet Milk. Cream also contains more calories than Pet Milk, which is something to remember if you are watching weight and waist lines.

DOG, CAT, OR HAMSTER MILK. WITH ENOUGH RADIATION, YOU WON'T KNOW THE DIFFERENCE EITHER.

RICE'N CREAM RING

3 cups cooked rice, chilled   ½ teas. vanilla
½ cup sugar   1 pt. double cream

Whip and sweeten half of the cream, add to the cooked chilled rice, folding it in. Put in a ring mold. Place in refrigerator until firm. At serving time, whip the remaining cream; unmold rice on serving plate, fill center with fluffy whipped cream. Serve with a pitcher of caramel sauce. Serves eight.

THIS LOOKS PRETTY APPETIZING...PROVIDED YOU'VE BEEN ADRIFT AT SEA FOR LONG ENOUGH.

ABOUT THE AUTHOR

Bryan Ballinger is uniquely qualified to be a professional self-published food commentator as he's been eating for as long as he can remember. You can reach him at bryan@kookycookery.com , or if he's lucky at a nearby potluck.

Made in the USA
San Bernardino, CA
14 December 2013